How to Analyze the Works of

FRANKLIN D. ROOSEVELT

by Mari Kesselring

ABDO
Publishing Company

Essential Critiques

How to Analyze the Works of

FRANKLIN D. ROOSEVELT

by Mari Kesselring

Content Consultant: Mary E. Stuckey
Professor of Communication and Political Science,
Georgia State University

Credits

Printed in the United States of America,
North Mankato, Minnesota
092012
012013

 THIS BOOK CONTAINS AT LEAST 10% RECYCLED MATERIALS.

Editor: Lauren Coss
Series Designer: Marie Tupy

Library of Congress Cataloging-in-Publication Data
Kesselring, Mari.
  How to analyze the works of Franklin D. Roosevelt / Mari Kesselring.
    p. cm. -- (Essential critiques)
Includes bibliographical references and index.
ISBN 978-1-61783-643-5
1. Roosevelt, Franklin D.--(Franklin Delano)--1882-1945--Criticism and interpretation--Juvenile literature. 2. Presidents--United States--Juvenile literature
3. Speeches, addresses, etc., American--Juvenile literature. I. Title.
973.917--dc14

2012946247

Table of Contents

Chapter 1   Introduction to Critiques   6

Chapter 2   A Closer Look at Franklin D. Roosevelt   12

Chapter 3   An Overview of "Fear Itself"   20

Chapter 4   How to Apply Biographical Criticism to "Fear Itself"   28

Chapter 5   An Overview of "On Drought Conditions"   40

Chapter 6   How to Apply Marxist Criticism to "On Drought
             Conditions"   48

Chapter 7   An Overview of "Four Freedoms"   58

Chapter 8   How to Apply Rhetorical Criticism to "Four Freedoms"   66

Chapter 9   An Overview of "A Date Which Will Live in Infamy"   78

Chapter 10   How to Apply Listener-Response Criticism to
             "A Date Which Will Live in Infamy"   84

You Critique It   96

Timeline   98

Glossary   100

Bibliography of Works and Criticism   102

Resources   104

Source Notes   106

Index   110

About the Author   112

Chapter

1

Introduction to Critiques

What Is Critical Theory?

What do you usually do when you read a book or essay or listen to a speech? You probably absorb the specific language style of the work. You also consider the point the speaker or writer is trying to convey. Yet these are only a few of many possible ways of understanding and appreciating a speech or piece of writing. What if you are interested in delving more deeply? You might want to learn more about the writer or speaker and how his or her personal background is reflected in the work. Or you might want to examine what the work says about society—how it depicts the roles of women and minorities, for example. If so, you have entered the realm of critical theory.

Critical theory helps you learn how art, literature, music, theater, film, politics, and other endeavors either support or challenge the way society behaves. Critical theory is the evaluation and interpretation of a work using different philosophies, or schools of thought. Critical theory can be used to understand all types of cultural works.

There are many different critical theories. Each theory asks you to look at the work from a different perspective. Some theories address social issues, while others focus on the writer's or speaker's life or the time period in which the work was created. For example, the critical theory that asks how an author's life affected the work is called biographical criticism. Other common schools of criticism include historical criticism, feminist criticism, psychological criticism, and New Criticism, which examines a work solely within the context of the work itself.

What Is the Purpose of Critical Theory?

Critical theory can open your mind to new ways of thinking. It can help you evaluate a piece of writing or a speech from a new perspective, directing your attention to issues and messages you may not otherwise recognize in a work. For example, applying feminist criticism to an essay may make you aware of female stereotypes perpetuated in the work. Applying a critical theory to a speech helps you learn about the person who gave it or the society that heard it. You can also explore how the work is perceived by current cultures.

How Do You Apply Critical Theory?

You conduct a critique when you use a critical theory to examine and question a work. The theory you choose is a lens through which you can view the work, or a springboard for asking questions about the work. Applying a critical theory helps you think critically about the work. You are free to question the work and make assertions about it. If you choose to examine an essay using biographical criticism, for example, you want to know how the writer's personal background or education inspired or shaped the work. You could explore why the writer was drawn to the subject. For instance, are there any parallels between points raised in the essay and details from the writer's life?

Forming a Thesis

Ask your question and find answers in the work or other related materials. Then you can create a thesis. The thesis is the key point in your critique. It is your argument about the work based on the tenets, or beliefs, of the theory you are using. For example, if you are using biographical criticism to ask how the writer's life inspired the work, your thesis could be worded as follows: Writer Teng Xiong, raised in refugee camps in Southeast Asia, drew upon her experiences to write the essay "No Home for Me."

> **How to Make a Thesis Statement**
>
> In a critique, a thesis statement typically appears at the end of the introductory paragraph. It is usually only one sentence long and states the author's main idea.

Providing Evidence

Once you have formed a thesis, you must provide evidence to support it. Evidence might take the form of examples and quotations from the work itself—such as excerpts from an essay. Articles about the essay or personal interviews with the writer might also support your ideas. You may wish to address what other critics have written about the work. Quotes from these individuals may help support your claim. If you find any quotes or examples that contradict your thesis, you will need to create an argument against them. For instance: <u>Many critics have pointed to the essay "No Home for Me" as detailing only the powerless circumstances Xiong faced. However, in the paragraphs focused on her emigration to the United States, Xiong clearly depicts herself as someone who can shape her own future.</u>

How to Support a Thesis Statement

A critique should include several arguments. Arguments support a thesis claim. An argument is one or two sentences long and is supported by evidence from the work being discussed.

Organize the arguments into paragraphs. These paragraphs make up the body of the critique.

In This Book

In this book, you will read summaries of famous speeches by President Franklin Delano Roosevelt, each followed by a critique. Each critique will use one theory and apply it to one speech. Critical thinking sections will give you a chance to consider other theses and questions about the work. Did you agree with the author's application of the theory? What other questions are raised by the thesis and its arguments? You can also find out what other critics think about each speech. Then, in the You Critique It section in the final pages of this book, you will have an opportunity to create your own critique.

Look for the Guides

Throughout the chapters that analyze the works, thesis statements have been highlighted. The box next to the thesis helps explain what questions are being raised about the work. Supporting arguments have been underlined. The boxes next to the arguments help explain how these points support the thesis. Look for these guides throughout each critique.

Franklin Delano Roosevelt was a strong leader during some of the country's most difficult times.

2

A Closer Look at Franklin D. Roosevelt

Franklin D. Roosevelt is one of history's most famous leaders. He served nearly four terms as president of the United States, more than any other president before or after him. Roosevelt led the country through some of its most challenging periods, including the Great Depression and World War II (1939–1945). His policies, along with his compassionate and optimistic attitude, made him popular with many Americans.

Growing Up

Franklin Delano Roosevelt was born in Hyde Park, New York, to James and Sara Delano Roosevelt on January 30, 1882. Both of Franklin's parents came from wealthy families, and Franklin had no siblings. As a result, his parents had the means to provide him with private tutors while he was growing up.

As a child, Franklin faced high expectations. His mother kept him on a strict schedule, requiring him to study every day. In 1896, when he was 14 years old, Franklin began attending Groton, a Massachusetts boarding school for boys. At school, he became interested in helping those less fortunate than himself. In 1900, Franklin began college at Harvard University in Cambridge, Massachusetts.

After graduation, Roosevelt went on to study law at Columbia Law School in September 1904. He also began courting Anna Eleanor Roosevelt, known as Eleanor. She was the niece of newly elected president Theodore Roosevelt, who was Roosevelt's cousin. Eleanor and Roosevelt married on March 17, 1905. Throughout the next 11 years, the couple would have six children together.

Entering Politics

In 1907, Roosevelt passed the New York bar exam and became a lawyer. However, Roosevelt soon decided he was more interested in politics than law. In 1910, Roosevelt ran for the New York State Senate as a Democrat. He won the election easily and was reelected in 1912. Then, in 1913, Roosevelt left his senatorial position when President Woodrow Wilson appointed him assistant secretary of the navy. Roosevelt held this position throughout President Wilson's two terms in office.

In 1920, Roosevelt was nominated for vice president with Democratic presidential hopeful and Ohio governor James Cox. Although the Republican candidate, Warren Harding, won the election, Roosevelt gained valuable experience on the campaign trail.

Trouble and Triumph

Roosevelt seemed to be on his way to a promising political career. In August 1921, Roosevelt and his family were vacationing on Campobello Island off the coast of Maine. Roosevelt was suddenly stricken with poliomyelitis, or polio. The disease left his legs paralyzed. Roosevelt tried everything his doctors recommended in an attempt to try to regain the full use of his legs. Despite these efforts, Roosevelt never walked unaided again.

Due to prejudices against people with disabilities at the time and a lack of medical assistance to deal with Roosevelt's new physical challenges, many people believed Roosevelt's political career was over. But Roosevelt had other ideas. Supported by Eleanor and his aide Louis Howe, Roosevelt was determined to work hard to get back into politics.

Although Roosevelt never walked again without assistance, he became an expert at hiding the effects of his paralysis. He could walk a few steps when wearing heavy metal braces on his legs and leaning on a cane or someone's arm. Roosevelt also began making frequent trips to Warm Springs, Georgia, where natural hot springs helped his condition. While in Warm Springs, Roosevelt got a firsthand look at the poverty in the rural town. Some scholars believe this experience with poverty made him more compassionate toward struggling families during the Depression.

In 1924, Roosevelt was chosen to speak at the Democratic National Convention. This was a sign there was still hope for his political career. In 1928, Roosevelt was elected governor of New York, and he was reelected in 1930. This time, he set his sights even higher. He began campaigning for the presidency of the United States.

Bringing Hope and Change

Roosevelt was elected president in 1932 in a near-landslide victory. The United States was at the height of the Great Depression, a period of economic distress following a stock market crash in 1929. When Roosevelt took office, the unemployment rate was nearly 25 percent. Roosevelt quickly took action to raise the spirits of Americans and improve the state of the country. He closed banks and began what he called New Deal programs. Through the New Deal, Roosevelt created various government-run agencies to assist with issues such as regulating the stock market and helping unemployed Americans. Roosevelt's popularity soared. He was reelected in 1936 by a landslide, and he was elected again in 1940, although this time by a smaller margin.

Wartime President

During his third term, Roosevelt focused more on foreign affairs. World War II had broken out in Europe when German forces attacked Poland in September 1939. At first, most Americans did not want to get involved in the war. Then, on December 7, 1941, Japanese forces carried out a surprise attack on Pacific naval bases, including Pearl Harbor, Hawaii. This attack took thousands of lives and destroyed many US military ships and airplanes. Roosevelt felt the only course of action was to join the war. At Roosevelt's request, the United States Congress declared war on Japan on December 8. The United States joined the Allied forces and officially entered World War II, partnered with France, Poland, the United Kingdom, the Soviet Union, and several other countries. Three days later, Germany and Italy, the countries allied with Japan in the coalition known as the Axis powers, declared war on the United States.

As president, Roosevelt played an active role in the war. He worked with military advisers to make strategic decisions. By early April 1945, victory in Europe seemed close at hand. But Roosevelt would not live to see the war's conclusion. The stress of the war had taken a toll on him. On April 12, 1945, Roosevelt suffered a fatal cerebral hemorrhage. He was buried at his estate in Hyde Park. Several weeks later, on May 8, the war ended in Europe with an Allied victory. A few months later, on September 2, 1945, Japan surrendered. World War II was over.

Roosevelt was president during some of the most challenging times in US history. He led the country through economic turmoil and a world war. Today, historians consider him to be one of the most popular presidents in US history. Roosevelt's legacy will not soon be forgotten.

Roosevelt was buried on April 15, 1945, just weeks before World War II ended in Europe.

Roosevelt's stirring "Fear Itself" speech was designed to give hope to Americans suffering during the Great Depression.

3

An Overview of "Fear Itself"

Historical Context

Roosevelt gave his "Fear Itself" speech on Inauguration Day 1933 as he began his first term as president. The United States was in the middle of the Great Depression. The situation in the country had been worsening for the past three years. Millions of people were unemployed and unable to find work. Conditions were so dire that some people were even dying of starvation.

After being disappointed by the efforts of the previous president, Herbert Hoover, many Americans hoped Roosevelt could help change the state of the country. Although speechwriter and advisor Raymond Moley wrote Roosevelt's speech, Roosevelt tweaked it to ensure he believed in the message it delivered. In the speech, Roosevelt made

Assistant Secretary of State Raymond Moley, *left*, advised Roosevelt, *right*, and played a large role in crafting Roosevelt's speeches.

it clear he wanted to restore hope for Americans, but he was not above placing blame on the institutions he felt had contributed to the Great Depression. As Americans listened in on their radios, Roosevelt addressed the nation.

Tough Times

Roosevelt begins his speech by acknowledging the tough times the United States is facing. He says he wants to be truthful with the American people about the state of their country. But Roosevelt also encourages his listeners with the now-famous line,

"Let me assert my firm belief that the only thing we have to fear is fear itself—nameless, unreasoning, unjustified terror which paralyzes needed efforts to convert retreat into advance."[1] Roosevelt explains that throughout history, Americans have faced many challenges. In these moments, Roosevelt asserts, American leaders attempting to help the nation have had the support of the American people. He hopes he can expect such support from Americans in the coming days. Then, to the thunderous applause of the audience, Roosevelt notes he will not hesitate to harness more power in order to help the nation.

The Problems

Roosevelt goes on to explain that though Americans face common difficulties, their challenges deal only with material things. He explains that the financial problems affect the country as well as individual families. He acknowledges that thousands of families are struggling due to job loss and lack of income. Many people have lost their life savings. Roosevelt also recognizes the problems of poor job security and low wages for those who are employed. He says, "Only a foolish optimist can deny the dark

realities of the moment."[2] Roosevelt understands
this is a critical moment for the country. But
he then reminds his listeners of the point he
raised earlier: the problems facing the country
concern material things. These problems can
be conquered. Additionally, Roosevelt reminds
Americans they have many reasons to be thankful,
especially compared to their forefathers, who faced
worse challenges.

Finding Solutions

Finally, Roosevelt begins offering his own
solutions to the economic crisis facing the United
States. He believes the country can be restored
if people work for social good rather than for
monetary profit. Roosevelt calls on Americans to
learn to work for the joy of completing a task rather
than for increasing their own material wealth. He
claims the Depression has taught people not to be
selfish. The crisis has schooled them to think about
the good of their community and fellow citizens.
Roosevelt believes people need to recognize that
material wealth is not a measure of true value.
Rather, Roosevelt upholds ideals of honesty,
honor, obligation, protection, and unselfish action.

Roosevelt claims in addition to changing their way of thinking, Americans and their government need to take action immediately to try to fix the nation's economic problems.

Roosevelt next shifts into discussing what he will do as president to enact change. He believes the most important task is putting citizens to work again. He proposes accomplishing this by empowering the government to create jobs for unemployed citizens. These unemployed Americans will work on projects that can improve the country as a whole. Roosevelt also hopes to rebalance the economy so industrial areas are not overpopulated. He recognizes the US government also needs to consider rural populations in the relief efforts. Roosevelt states current relief efforts are poorly organized. He plans to arrange government relief efforts so assistance will be equal around the country. Additionally, to avoid another depression, Roosevelt wants to give the government more control in regulating banks.

Roosevelt also touches briefly on world policy. He explains that he wants the United States to be viewed as a good neighbor to other countries. He wants the country to honor and respect its agreements with other governments. Still, the country's greatest obligation needs to be improving itself. While Roosevelt wants to restore world trade, his first priority will be focusing on national recovery. He believes this is the quickest path to success for the country.

Roosevelt then calls on the American people to unite and make sacrifices for one another. He believes the American people now understand how they are all connected. Roosevelt asserts he will lead this united group of Americans to attack the common problems they all face. He explains that Americans should feel obligated to work to make the country better with the same support they would give their country if it were at war.

Roosevelt reminds his audience that the US government is allowed to make changes to help Americans through difficult times. This flexibility will help the country to meet the challenges it is now facing. Roosevelt believes this ability to change the way the government functions in order to address growing national needs is the strength of the Constitution. He also believes this is the reason the country has been so successful in the past. He acknowledges that Congress has the ability to monitor and reject the programs a president wants to implement. Roosevelt explains that if Congress blocks his attempts at aiding the country, he will ask for greater power as president.

Roosevelt likens his fight against the Great Depression to a war against a foreign foe. He needs more executive power, just as the president is often granted additional powers during wartime. But Roosevelt also wants to make it clear the American people and US democracy have not failed. Rather, he believes they have done the correct thing by choosing Roosevelt to lead their country in this time of need.

Finally, Roosevelt says by electing him president, Americans have asked him to direct them during this national turmoil. Roosevelt accepts this gift the American people have given him. He closes his speech by asking for a blessing from God to protect the American people and guide him in his leadership.

Roosevelt's personal struggles, including his disability, are reflected in his "Fear Itself" speech.

4

How to Apply Biographical Criticism to "Fear Itself"

No.2

What Is Biographical Criticism?

Biographical criticism focuses on the ways in which aspects of an author's life are revealed in and affect his or her work. A biographical critic will consider a speech or story in light of the author's past experiences and influences. Biographical criticism can reveal things about the speaker's life even if he or she was not the author of the speech. For example, although speechwriter Moley actually wrote much of the "Fear Itself" speech, Roosevelt approved the speech and tweaked the language to ensure it reflected his own feelings and beliefs. Roosevelt then delivered the speech in a way that emphasized the parts he felt were most important.

Applying Biographical Criticism to "Fear Itself"

Roosevelt took the oath of office on March 4, 1933, during a time of great distress in the United States. After the stock market crash of 1929, the Great Depression took hold of the nation's economy. Banks closed and unemployment was the worst it had ever been in US history. The country was in need of a strong leader who would improve the situation in the United States and give the country back the hope and determination it had lost as the Depression dragged on.

In addition to the trials facing the country, Roosevelt had already been through many personal trials by this time in his life. In August 1921, Roosevelt had been suddenly stricken with polio. The disease left him partially paralyzed. He was unable to walk without assistance for the rest of his life. However, Roosevelt remained determined to continue his career in politics.

In his 1933 inaugural speech, more than ten years after losing the full use of his legs, Roosevelt encouraged the nation to have a similar determination and courage during some of its darkest days. Roosevelt's optimistic and determined approach to meeting the challenges of his disability is reflected in his 1933 inaugural speech.

In this speech, Roosevelt asserts his beliefs about overcoming fear. These beliefs were greatly influenced by his personal experiences as a disabled man. Eleanor referred to the winter after Roosevelt contracted polio as "the most trying" time of her life.[1] Roosevelt reportedly feared he would die during this period. He claimed to be bothered by the floral-patterned wallpaper in the room he was staying in. It reminded him of a tomb. But Roosevelt learned to conquer his fear. Eleanor later remarked regarding her husband's illness, "I know that he had real fear when he was first taken ill, but he learned to surmount it. After that I never heard him say he was afraid of anything."[2]

Thesis Statement

The author's thesis states: "Roosevelt's optimistic and determined approach to meeting the challenges of his disability is reflected in his 1933 inaugural speech." The author focuses on the way Roosevelt's personal trials are reflected in the speech.

Argument One

The author first focuses on Roosevelt's ideas about fear as they are presented in the speech. The first argument states: "In this speech, Roosevelt asserts his beliefs about overcoming fear. These beliefs were greatly influenced by his personal experiences as a disabled man."

Eleanor Roosevelt
supported her
husband as he
came to terms
with his disability.

Roosevelt's most famous line in this speech is
"Let me assert my firm belief that the only thing we
have to fear is fear itself—nameless, unreasoning,
unjustified terror which paralyzes needed efforts

to convert retreat into advance."[3] When Roosevelt spoke to the country about fear and how it can be conquered, he was speaking from personal experience. He had already learned how to conquer his own fear. In fact, in his speech, Roosevelt even puts special emphasis on the word *fear*. Roosevelt pauses for a long moment after saying, "The only thing we have to fear is," before continuing with the words "fear itself."[4] Roosevelt then categorizes fear as "nameless, unreasoning, unjustified terror," speaking these words quickly, as if they are trivial to him.[5] Having vanquished his own fear, Roosevelt was ready to be brave for the American people.

Roosevelt's positive tone in the speech despite the trauma the country was facing reflects his positive attitude toward his physical challenges. Early in his speech, Roosevelt points out that the country's concerns have to do with material issues, and things could be much worse. He states, "We face our common difficulties. They concern, thank God, only material things."[6] Roosevelt faced difficulties that were

> **Argument Two**
> Next, the author turns to how Roosevelt defines the country's problems in light of his own experiences. The second argument is: "Roosevelt's positive tone in the speech despite the trauma the country was facing reflects his positive attitude toward his physical challenges."

greater than a loss of material possessions—he had lost his ability to walk. Even then, he remained largely optimistic about his life. In the months after he got sick, many of his friends were surprised at his positive attitude in the wake of his illness.

Roosevelt no doubt struggled with his disability, but he tried his best to put on a brave face. In his speech, Roosevelt reminds Americans, "We have still much to be thankful for."[7] In other parts of the speech, Roosevelt uses a much sterner tone, but he speaks these words in a lighthearted, almost cheerful fashion. This light tone reflects Roosevelt's naturally upbeat attitude. His doctors often commented on his positive attitude. Roosevelt maintained an optimistic attitude in the face of his challenges, and as president, this attitude helped him lead a nation facing a rough road.

The determination and discipline in Roosevelt's speech reflects his resolve to overcome society's stigma against handicapped people. In the speech, Roosevelt announces, "If we are to go

Argument Three

The author presents the third argument: "The determination and discipline in Roosevelt's speech reflects his resolve to overcome society's stigma against handicapped people." This section focuses on Roosevelt's determination in both his political career and his personal life.

forward, we must move as a trained and loyal army willing to sacrifice for the good of a common discipline, because without such discipline, no progress is made."[8] Roosevelt speaks of a common discipline for Americans that will help rebuild the country's economy.

In his own life, Roosevelt was determined to rebuild his career in politics after losing the use of his legs. In the early twentieth century, it was rare for a physically handicapped person to succeed in politics. But despite the stigma of his illness, Roosevelt was resolute. The son of a Roosevelt family friend once commented, "Having handled [polio], [Roosevelt] probably thought there wasn't anything he couldn't deal with."[9] Roosevelt's determination and discipline paid off. In expressing the value of determination to the country, Roosevelt is speaking from personal experience. He uses the qualities that helped him come to terms with his illness to help heal an ailing country.

Roosevelt's inaugural speech on March 4, 1933, was meant to encourage and empower the

> **Conclusion**
>
> In the conclusion, the author restates the thesis, now backed up by the supporting arguments. The conclusion also leaves the reader with a new thought: Roosevelt upheld the highest of hopes for himself and the United States.

nation to rebuild itself in the midst of the Great Depression. By this time, Roosevelt had been shaped by his experiences with polio and had learned how to live without the full use of his legs. The words in his inaugural address, as well as the way he delivered them, echo Roosevelt's own core beliefs but are framed to fit the needs of the country he was elected to lead. Roosevelt's determination to succeed was always strong. He had high expectations for himself and the country he led. These expectations helped lead Roosevelt to the presidency, and they helped move the United States toward a better future.

Thinking Critically about "Fear Itself"

Now it is your turn to assess the critique.
Consider these questions:

1. The author argues Roosevelt's experiences with polio are revealed in his "Fear Itself" speech to the nation. Do you agree with the author's thesis? Why or why not?

2. Are any other details from Roosevelt's biography reflected in the speech? What are they?

3. What was the most convincing argument the author made? What was the weakest? Why?

Other Approaches

This essay represents only one way of applying biographical criticism to Roosevelt's 1933 inaugural "Fear Itself" speech. Other approaches might look at different aspects of Roosevelt's life entirely. The following are two other approaches to the speech using biographical criticism. One approach deals with how Roosevelt's optimistic attitude is revealed in the speech. The other focuses on how Roosevelt's religious beliefs at that time are highlighted in the speech.

Positive President

People around Roosevelt often remarked on how good-humored he always seemed to be. His friends and political acquaintances knew him as a cheerful and optimistic person. In his "Fear Itself" speech, Roosevelt acknowledges the difficulties that lay ahead for the nation. However, he takes care to focus on the positive side of things as well. He points out, "In every dark hour of our national life, a leadership of frankness and vigor has met with that understanding and support of the people themselves which is essential to victory."[10]

One example of a thesis statement for a critique that takes this approach might be: Roosevelt's positive attitude about life is reflected in the hopeful tone of his 1933 inaugural speech.

Chosen by God

In the "Fear Itself" speech, Roosevelt calls upon God to strengthen him and the American people. He even quotes a line from the Bible. Some scholars speculate that Roosevelt, like many Americans at the time, believed God had chosen the United States to be his faithful country. Roosevelt sometimes even seemed to believe God had chosen Roosevelt's path in politics for him. He believed God would test him to see if he would be able to lead the country. Roosevelt's belief and faith in God, particularly during his early years as president, is reflected in his "Fear Itself" speech.

A thesis statement for a critique dealing with Roosevelt's religious beliefs could be: Roosevelt's belief that he was chosen by God to lead the United States is revealed in his 1933 inaugural speech.

Essential Critiques

Roosevelt used his regular fireside chats to connect with Americans listening in their homes.

An Overview of "On Drought Conditions"

Historical Context

After taking presidential office for his first term in 1933, Roosevelt quickly began implementing programs to help his country recover from the Great Depression. Roosevelt also wanted to keep the public informed on how the recovery process was going. On March 12, 1933, Roosevelt started giving regular radio speeches he called fireside chats. Americans listened to these addresses from living rooms across the country. In the speeches, Roosevelt explained the reasoning behind certain government actions and addressed public concerns. Using this medium, Roosevelt was able to reach millions of Americans.

There was plenty for Roosevelt to discuss with Americans during these chats. In his fireside chat

"On Drought Conditions," Roosevelt discusses one of the biggest issues during the Great Depression. In the early 1930s, a period of drought combined with poor farming practices in plains states such as Oklahoma, Texas, and Kansas brought on devastating erosion. Along with huge dust storms, this led to widespread crop failure. The area affected became known as the dust bowl.

With crops failing and farms facing foreclosure, thousands of dust bowl refugees left their farms and relocated to large cities. These former farmers often continued struggling even after leaving the dust bowl. In many cities, work was already scarce. Farmer refugees, called *Okies*, were not welcomed and often could not find work. Roosevelt's administration put relief programs into place for struggling farmers. This was one of many assistance programs created during the 1930s. In his speech "On Drought Conditions," Roosevelt updates the country on the recovery progress in the farming states.

Devastated by Drought

In his fireside chat with the nation on September 6, 1936, Roosevelt begins by explaining

he has just returned from a trip during which he visited nine states to view the effects of the drought for himself. Roosevelt paints a picture for his listeners of the destruction in these states. He recalls dried-up fields of wheat and pastures full of dead grass. The purpose of Roosevelt's trip was to look at the way government and local authorities were dealing with the problems caused by the drought and poverty in those states. Roosevelt explains that many farm families are suffering greatly as a result of the drought.

During the Great Depression, giant dust storms plagued the central United States.

Solutions

Roosevelt asserts that the dire situation in these farming states is not permanent. He explains it is the government's job to assist suffering farmers, many of whom come from generations of farm families. He proposes the government create jobs for people who have no other means to provide for themselves after losing their farms. These government-created jobs will last farmers through the winter. The farmers will then have money to restart their farms in the spring. Roosevelt adds that he has spoken with the governors of these states, and they fully support his plan. He also explains that since 1934, the government has been using emergency work programs in these areas to create jobs. The projects completed through these government-created jobs will also help prevent further farm disasters. For example, people working for these programs have created reservoirs, drilled wells, and made roads leading from farms to markets. The jobs the government is creating are helping build structures that will increase farming profits in the coming years.

Next, Roosevelt explains in detail why he feels it is important to assist farm families. Roosevelt believes more farmers will move to cities in search of work if they do not get help from the government. This will make it even more difficult to find work in the cities. He also believes city property values will decline. However, if the government steps in to help, Roosevelt believes the opposite will happen.

He explains the economy connects all workers in the nation. If farmers fail, he says, everyone will feel the effects. Roosevelt notes in addition to a short-term program to help farmers, the government is working on a long-term program that will regulate farming. This way farms can still function in the event of another drought. He wants farms to be able to survive and thrive even after a year of poor crops. Roosevelt goes on to explain that although these policies have been created on a national level, it is the job of local governments to carry them out. He notes that local farmers are cooperating in changing farming methods to make them more sustainable and profitable.

Labor Day

The president then reminds his listeners the next day is Labor Day. This is why he has chosen to speak about reemployment during this particular fireside chat. But Roosevelt also has another reason for choosing this topic. He wants to explain how important farming is to the national economy. He notes, "Dependable employment at fair wages is just as important to the people in the towns and cities as good farm income is to agriculture."[1]

Improvements

Roosevelt explains reemployment in industry has been increasing thanks to government programs similar to the one that has been assisting farmers. He notes when employers requested more current information about available workers, the government fulfilled their requests. A program called the US Employment Service has made records regarding citizens' past work experiences available to potential employers. This helps employers easily find people who match their needs. Roosevelt states he is allocating $2.5 million more to the Employment Service so employers can continue locating skilled workers. Roosevelt calls on all US workers and employers to take full advantage of this service.

Roosevelt returns to his discussion of Labor Day. He explains that all workers are equal in importance, no matter what type of work they do. All Americans have the same needs in an economic democracy. He notes Labor Day should symbolize hope this year. While the Fourth of July celebrates political freedom, Roosevelt wants Labor Day to symbolize the need for economic freedom.

Roosevelt meets with struggling farmers from Bismarck, North Dakota.

Some dust bowl farmers lost everything during the droughts of the mid-1930s.

6

How to Apply Marxist Criticism to "On Drought Conditions"

No.2

What Is Marxist Criticism?

Marxist criticism is named after Karl Marx, a German philosopher who lived in the mid-nineteenth century. Today, Marxist critics look at how a work relates to class. They might try to decide which class is represented in a certain work, or they might consider how the social class of the speaker factors into the work. They might also consider which class or classes a work supports. Using Marxist criticism can help a reader or listener understand social structures.

Applying Marxist Criticism to "On Drought Conditions"

Although many Americans suffered during the Great Depression, not everyone was struggling.

In general, upper-class Americans did not suffer from unemployment to the extent the middle and lower classes did. The upper class maintained the majority of its wealth despite the Depression. This created an even greater division between the upper and lower classes than what existed before the Depression. The upper class began resenting the lower class because Roosevelt paid for many of the New Deal programs by taxing people with an income, including the upper class. They also worried such programs gave the government too much power.

During these challenging times, Roosevelt had the difficult task of calming tensions between the classes while helping the country recover from the Depression. Roosevelt's "On Drought Conditions" fireside chat reflects his attempt to overturn upper-class prejudices against lower-class Americans and diminish the threat class struggle might pose to the country's recovery.

Thesis Statement

At the end of the first paragraph, the author states the thesis: "Roosevelt's 'On Drought Conditions' fireside chat reflects his attempt to overturn upper-class prejudices against lower-class Americans and diminish the threat class struggle might pose to the country's recovery." The author focuses on class prejudice and how it could slow the nation's recovery from the Depression.

Roosevelt's depiction of farm workers as moral and hardworking goes against the attitudes of the upper classes toward lower-class farmers at that time. During the Great Depression, many rural Americans moved to big cities to try to find jobs. Middle- and upper-class Americans already living in cities often disliked these rural newcomers. Because of this prejudice, not everyone was happy government money was being used to help farmers. In his chat, Roosevelt fights this view by asserting that farmers in the areas affected by the drought "do not want to be dependent on federal, state, or any other kind of charity."[1]

Roosevelt depicts farm families as being similar to families in urban areas that are also struggling: "Dependable employment at fair wages is just as important to the people in the towns and cities as good farm income is to agriculture."[2] Roosevelt's likening of these two groups is an attempt to raise the upper classes' opinions of the lower-class farmers. It reveals the prevalent lack of

> **Argument One**
>
> The first argument states: "Roosevelt's depiction of farm workers as moral and hardworking goes against the attitudes of the upper classes toward lower-class farmers at that time." The author proves the speech reveals prejudices against the lower class.

Argument Two

Next, the author discusses Roosevelt's attempts to diffuse class prejudice. The second argument states: "Roosevelt's explanation of how important the lower class is to the national economy is calculated to encourage support for the aid given to the lower class and to fight against existing prejudices."

Roosevelt heard firsthand about how the drought affected farm families in Julesburg, Colorado.

understanding and support for farm families.

Roosevelt's explanation of how important the lower class is to the national economy is calculated to encourage support for the aid given to the lower class and to fight against existing prejudices. Roosevelt directly ties the success of the lower class to the success of the upper class, explaining, "Healthy employment conditions stand equally with healthy agricultural conditions

as a buttress of national prosperity."[3] While the upper classes might have wanted to distance themselves from the poor farmers due to prejudice, Roosevelt links their welfare together. He asserts that wealthy Americans cannot prosper if farmers do not succeed. In order to defeat the Depression, Roosevelt needs wealthy Americans to support relief programs such as the ones occurring in the drought-affected areas.

Roosevelt ends his speech by encouraging a united, classless approach to national recovery. He tells his listeners that all workers, no matter their class, need to pull their weight to get the country out of the tough economic times. Roosevelt goes on to remind Americans the next day is Labor Day. Roosevelt stresses Labor Day is a national holiday that does not recognize class. He explains that the same freedoms need to be available to everyone regardless of class. Roosevelt supports a united America, explaining, "All American workers, brain workers and manual workers alike . . . know that our needs are one in building an orderly economic

> **Argument Three**
> The author presents the third argument: "Roosevelt ends his speech by encouraging a united, classless approach to national recovery." The author shows how Roosevelt attempts to promote a united nation.

democracy in which all can profit."[4] He asserts that the goal for all Americans, wealthy and poor alike, is the same—a recovered economy.

In his fireside chat "On Drought Conditions," Roosevelt's attempts to equalize and unite the classes to support the country's recovery reveal the underlying class prejudices and tensions he is trying to combat. Knowing the division between the wealthy and the poor often grows during times of extreme poverty such as the Great Depression, Roosevelt was well aware of this tension. While the United States would not become a classless society, Roosevelt's speech took steps toward uniting the country to a common purpose. He helped the American people understand that to succeed as a society, rich and poor would have to unite and work together.

> **Conclusion**
>
> In the conclusion, the author restates her thesis, now backed up by her supporting arguments. She also notes the political skills that allowed Roosevelt to recognize this class tension.

Thinking Critically about "On Drought Conditions"

Now it is your turn to assess the critique. Consider these questions:

1. The author's thesis argues Roosevelt's speech reveals class prejudices. Do you agree? What else might the speech reveal about the time period?

2. What sections of the critique do you believe were the most effective? Which were the least effective? Why?

3. A conclusion should summarize the thesis statements and arguments of a critique. It should also leave the reader with a new idea. Is this conclusion effective? Why or why not?

Other Approaches

This essay shows one way to apply Marxist criticism to Roosevelt's "On Drought Conditions" fireside chat. However, there are multiple ways to apply this type of criticism to the speech. The Great Depression is often studied using Marxist criticism. The following are two other approaches to critiquing this speech using Marxist criticism. The first focuses on how Roosevelt reveals the shame felt by people from various classes who were unable to maintain their class status. The second approach looks at how Roosevelt upholds the importance of work itself over a specific type of work.

The American Nightmare

During the Depression, many people who became unemployed and poverty stricken blamed themselves for their situations. Many felt guilty because they were not able to sustain the same quality of life for themselves and their families that they had enjoyed in past years. People whose families had been considered middle class for generations suddenly became lower-class families. In his "On Drought Conditions" fireside chat, it is clear Roosevelt is aware of the shame many of these Americans were feeling.

A possible thesis statement for a critique taking this approach might be: Roosevelt's reassuring fireside chat "On Drought Conditions" reveals his awareness of the shame many farmers and other workers felt when they were not able to maintain their economic status.

Equal Workers

Roosevelt's "On Drought Conditions" fireside chat discusses the importance of all US jobs to the economy. Roosevelt attacks the idea that certain professions should be considered more important than others. Even today many people feel some jobs are more important than others. This usually has to do with how much money a person makes in a particular career or how much power a person has in his or her job. This ideology, which was also common during the Depression, reinforces stereotypes about class.

A thesis statement for an essay that looks at these issues might be: Through the fireside chat "On Drought Conditions," Roosevelt attempts to portray all professions as interconnected and of equal importance to the country's success.

In Roosevelt's 1941 State of the Union address to Congress, Roosevelt discusses his concerns about the war that has been raging in Europe.

An Overview of "Four Freedoms"

Historical Context

By the start of his third term as president, Roosevelt had been weighing the necessity of US involvement in the conflict in Europe since the late 1930s. Many Americans wanted the United States to remain at peace. Some citizens and politicians maintained the United States should not ally with any of the countries involved in the conflict. They wanted to remain completely neutral. However, Roosevelt worried the threat in Europe would eventually make its way to the United States. Then, on September 3, 1939, after German troops marched into Poland, both Great Britain and France declared war on Germany. As German forces made more European conquests, Roosevelt prepared his nation for a war he now felt was inevitable. Although he still did not have full national support for entering the war, Roosevelt began building up national defenses and reinforcing political relationships with Great Britain and France. He wanted the United States to be in a strong position to enter the war if necessary.

As Roosevelt began his third term, the national debate on whether to remain neutral in the war had reached a breaking point. On January 6, 1941, Roosevelt gave one of the most famous speeches of his presidency. With the speech, Roosevelt firmly warned Americans about the prospect of war and what would happen if the nation were unprepared to meet the threat. The country was headed into a tumultuous period, and Roosevelt felt the United States could no longer remain neutral if it was threatened. He wanted Americans to be prepared in the event the United States chose to enter the war.

An Attack on Democracy

At the time of the "Four Freedoms" speech, the war in Europe had been going on for 16 months. Roosevelt begins his speech by asserting the "democratic way of life" is being "directly assailed" all over the world.[1] Roosevelt explains this attack on democracy is being accomplished through both force and corruption. He goes on to say the war in Europe is affecting nations around the globe. He proclaims the assaulting nations are challenging democracy and have become a threat to all countries, big and small.

Roosevelt then confirms that as president, he is acting on his "constitutional duty" to inform Congress about the condition of the United States in relation to the world.[2] He reports, "The future and the safety of our country and of our democracy are overwhelmingly involved in events far beyond our borders."[3] With this statement, Roosevelt claims the war in Europe threatens the United States despite its efforts to remain neutral.

An Unprepared America

Roosevelt goes on to explain that this war is being waged on four continents—Europe, Asia, Africa, and Australasia (today known as Oceania). He shares his concern that the democratic forces in these countries will be conquered. He refers to Norway—a nation whose seaports have been captured by German forces because it was not expecting an attack. Roosevelt compares Norway to "an unprepared America."[4] He explains the United States cannot survive by remaining peaceful in a warring world, and peace cannot keep the nation or its neighbors safe from attack.

Pending Attacks

Roosevelt next outlines potential threats to the United States. He explains his belief that the United States is not completely safe from an attack. He claims if the Axis powers win the war, the United States will surely be attacked. Roosevelt acknowledges that many people feel the United States is immune to attacks because oceans surround it. He adds that as long as the British navy is patrolling the oceans, the United States will be safe, and even if the British navy should crumble, an enemy would be foolish to try to attack by sea.

However, Roosevelt cautions an offensive cannot be completely ruled out. He makes his main point: "As long as the aggressor nations maintain the offensive, they—not we—will choose the time and the place and the method of their attack."[5] In this way, Roosevelt warns Americans of the possibility of a surprise attack. He stresses that because of this danger, his annual message to

Congress is very important this year. He explains the US government has a great responsibility to keep the nation safe from its enemies.

German forces march into the Norwegian capital of Oslo on May 2, 1940, nearly one month after the initial German invasion of Norway.

The Policy

Finally, Roosevelt outlines his national policy. He explains the nation needs to focus "almost exclusively" on its enemies.[6] The first thing the nation needs to address, according to Roosevelt, is national defense. He asserts his belief that American citizens are now asking their government to take this step. Secondly, Roosevelt believes the United States has an obligation to support the nations that are fighting the challengers of democracy. Roosevelt reminds Americans it is these nations that keep war away from the Western Hemisphere. By showing its support for these countries, the United States will express its respect for the democratic cause and improve its own security. Finally, Roosevelt asserts the United States will not be peaceful simply as a means of satisfying its aggressors. The United States needs to understand peace cannot be accepted in place of freedom, and force may soon be necessary.

The Four Freedoms

In closing, Roosevelt outlines the four freedoms that make his speech famous. Before introducing them, he explains, "In the future days, which we seek to make secure, we look forward to a world founded upon four essential human freedoms."[7] Roosevelt then outlines the rights he believes every individual should have in a new world order. The first freedom is speech and expression. The freedom to worship God is the second freedom. The third freedom is the freedom from want.

Roosevelt explains the need for making economic adjustments that will eliminate the need for conflict over resources. This will lead to worldwide peace. The fourth and final freedom is freedom from fear. Roosevelt explains this can be achieved by reducing weapons so nations will not be able to attack their neighbors.

Roosevelt asserts these goals can be achieved within this generation's lifetime. He explains the future he has described is the opposite of what the United States' enemies are fighting for. Roosevelt believes that in this new world order, the country will be able to face threats without fear. He notes the United States has been in continual evolution since it was founded. The country has always adjusted to the changing world without violence or oppression. He explains, "The world order which we seek is the cooperation of free countries, working together in a friendly, civilized society."[8] He closes by explaining that for this moral goal, the only result is victory.

Roosevelt's powerful rhetoric helped persuade audiences to see his point of view.

How to Apply Rhetorical Criticism to "Four Freedoms"

No.2

What Is Rhetorical Criticism?

Rhetorical criticism helps a reader understand communication by taking a closer look at the structure and persuasive techniques of a work such as a speech. Rhetorical critics go further than simply deciding whether they liked or were persuaded by a speech. They also examine why they enjoyed the speech or felt moved to action by it. By becoming aware of the techniques used in an effective speech or other work, critics can become more successful communicators themselves. They can also more easily recognize when they are being persuaded by a speech and outline what exactly is causing them to alter their opinion on a given topic.

When looking at different persuasive elements in a work, critics often examine the three categories

of persuasion—ethos, pathos, and logos. The
Greek philosopher Aristotle studied rhetoric and
was the first to define these categories, which he
called *appeals*.

Ethos is defined as an author or speaker trying
to gain the respect of the audience by asserting her
or his authority on a subject. People are more likely
to agree with someone who has an authoritative
position relating to a given topic. The second
appeal, pathos, refers to an author appealing to the
listener's or reader's emotions. An author may use
imagery or emotional language to try to gain the
audience's sympathies for his or her cause. The
final appeal is logos. Logos is defined as an author
putting forth an argument in a logical way. The
author will try to prove his or her point by giving
clear, logical examples that support the claim. Many
works employ all three of these appeals to some
degree, but they will usually lean more heavily on
one of the three.

Applying Rhetorical Criticism to "Four Freedoms"

As Roosevelt gave his speech on
January 6, 1941, there is little doubt he was
concerned about the threat facing his country.

He believed the war being waged in Europe would eventually draw the United States in. Roosevelt knew the country needed to prepare for conflict, and he needed the support of the American people in these preparations. But many Americans were still resistant to joining the battle. People across the country were debating whether the country should involve itself in a war that seemed so far away. Roosevelt's persuasive "Four Freedoms" speech employs Aristotle's appeals of pathos and logos in an attempt to sway the American public from its antiwar stance.

Throughout the speech, Roosevelt manipulates the audience's emotions by using imagery that provokes fear. First, Roosevelt uses such imagery to depict the United States. He explains it is immature and false to believe "that an unprepared America, single-handed, and

Thesis Statement

At the end of the first paragraph, the author states the thesis: "Roosevelt's persuasive 'Four Freedoms' speech employs Aristotle's appeals of pathos and logos in an attempt to sway the American public from its antiwar stance." This critique shows how Roosevelt uses pathos and logos to make a persuasive argument.

Argument One

The author first focuses on how Roosevelt uses a pathos to make the audience feel fearful in order to persuade them to support his stance on US involvement in the war. The first argument states: "Throughout the speech, Roosevelt manipulates the audience's emotions by using imagery that provokes fear."

Roosevelt references an eagle in his speech to appeal to Americans' patriotism.

with one hand tied behind its back, can hold off the whole world."[1] This visual makes the United States look weak and impaired. Roosevelt personifies and describes the nation as having one hand tied behind its back, unable to adequately fight or defend itself. Such an image would likely make the audience feel fearful and insecure about their safety. Roosevelt goes on to produce another fearful image. He presents an image of an eagle, the national bird and a symbol of American strength, explaining that some selfish people "would clip the wings of the

American eagle in order to feather their own nests."[2]
The image of an eagle with clipped wings, unable to
fly, reinforces the idea of a helpless United States.
Once again, the thought of being undefended or
impaired against foes would be a fearful notion
for Americans.

   After stirring up the audience's emotions,
Roosevelt changes tactics for the middle part of
his speech. In this section of the
speech, Roosevelt uses logic
to explain the country's dire
situation in a calculated, clear
manner. In explaining why the
United States has reason to
fear, Roosevelt gives examples
of surprise attacks that have
already happened in Europe.
He specifically references an attack on Norway's
seaports. By backing up his concerns with examples
of what has happened in other countries unprepared
for attacks, Roosevelt makes a logical argument.
He asserts as long as the United States remains
defensive rather than offensive, the enemy "will
choose the time and the place and the method of
their attack."[3] This is a logically true and unarguable

> **Argument Two**
> The second argument is: "In
> this section of the speech,
> Roosevelt uses logic to explain
> the country's dire situation in
> a calculated, clear manner."
> The author now shows how
> Roosevelt makes a strong
> argument using logic, or logos.

statement. If the United States is not planning to attack anyone, any attack that occurs would be one planned by US enemies. It would be carried out in the way these enemies chose. Roosevelt's logical argument, aided by the emotional appeal with which he opened the speech, creates a strong and convincing core for the speech.

As the speech draws to a close, Roosevelt again appeals to Americans' fears. But he also speaks to their pride by saying their country will surely be triumphant should it get involved in the conflict. Near the end of the speech, Roosevelt delivers perhaps his most graphic, frightening imagery. He explains the country's enemies "seek to create with the crash of a bomb."[4] He means the nation's enemies are using force to create their own empire. Roosevelt makes this image even more disturbing by using the word *crash*. Rather than just explaining that the United States' foes will attack with force, he invokes the sound of a bomb going off. This strong

> **Argument Three**
> The author presents the third argument: "As the speech draws to a close, Roosevelt again appeals to Americans' fears. But he also speaks to their pride by saying their country will surely be triumphant should it get involved in the conflict." Here the author shows how Roosevelt makes his listeners feel pride in their country, ending his speech on a positive note.

language is designed to make the listener fearful of the threat facing the nation.

But Roosevelt goes on to evoke feelings of pride in his listeners. Roosevelt promotes a new world order that is moral. He explains that such a society will be able to face threats "without fear."[5] In this way, he speaks to his listeners' pride by indicating they are a part of this moral society. He further appeals to the pride US citizens have in their country's history. He notes, "Since the beginning of our American history, we have been engaged in change—in a perpetual peaceful revolution."[6]

A billboard in 1941 encourages Americans to support the United Services Organization (USO), a group dedicated to supporting members of the US military as the nation headed toward war.

Roosevelt calls for the nation to be united through this common purpose. He is attempting to evoke emotions of triumph in the face of adversity. He explains, "Our strength is our unity of purpose."[7] Finally, Roosevelt closes by affirming that Americans should feel proud of their nation's goals. He states, "To that high concept there can be no end save victory."[8] Roosevelt asserts the United States' goal is so moral that even if it enters and loses the war, the country will achieve a moral victory.

Conclusion

The conclusion is the final paragraph of the critique. In the conclusion, the author summarizes how Roosevelt was successful in creating a strong, persuasive argument. The author also notes how important it was for Roosevelt to feel Americans understood the threats facing their nation.

Roosevelt's "Four Freedoms" speech came at a critical time in US history. The country was locked in an intense debate about whether it should declare war on the Axis powers or remain neutral. Roosevelt believed it was time for the United States to join the war, but he needed the American people behind him. By mixing fear with national pride and backing up his arguments with logical statements, Roosevelt makes a strong case for war.

Thinking Critically about "Four Freedoms"

Now it is your turn to assess the critique. Consider these questions:

1. The author argues Roosevelt uses Aristotle's appeals of pathos and logos to make a strong argument for entering the war. Do you think Roosevelt also employs an ethos appeal in this speech? If so, how?

2. What parts of this essay did you find to be the most and the least convincing? Why? What could you add to the arguments to make them stronger?

3. The author asserts that with this speech, Roosevelt was attempting to gain the support of the US public. Why might Roosevelt want or need this support? Do these reasons come through in his speech?

Other Approaches

This essay is just one way to apply rhetorical criticism to Roosevelt's "Four Freedoms" speech. There are multiple ways to critique the speech using rhetorical criticism. The following are two other approaches. One approach focuses on how Roosevelt uses Aristotle's ethos appeal. The second approach claims Roosevelt is attempting to be informative rather than persuasive with his speech.

Authority

Early in his speech, Roosevelt explains that in giving his address to the nation, he is performing his "constitutional duty."[9] Roosevelt uses his executive authority to help him make this argument. After all, as the president of the United States, Roosevelt's opinion likely carries some weight with the American people. Roosevelt seems aware of this throughout the speech and uses it to his advantage.

A thesis statement for a critique that takes this approach could be: Roosevelt uses his authoritative position as president of the United States in an attempt to sway the public away from its antiwar stance.

To Inform

Rhetorical criticism has a broad range of approaches. Not all applications of rhetorical criticism use Aristotle's appeals to analyze a work. Another school of rhetorical criticism looks at how a speech informs the audience of the speaker's opinion rather than how it might be trying to persuade them to accept the speaker's point of view. Roosevelt might have hoped that as he was the nation's president, many other Americans would share his opinions.

A thesis statement for a critique claiming Roosevelt's aim is to inform the people of his opinion could read: Throughout the speech, Roosevelt explains what he believes the country needs to do, but he never directly calls on Americans to take specific action. This suggests his ultimate goal is to inform and warn Americans about the threat of war rather than spurring them to action.

On December 8, 1941, Roosevelt gave one of his most famous speeches in reaction to the Japanese military attack on Pearl Harbor in Hawaii.

An Overview of "A Date Which Will Live in Infamy"

Historical Context

As Roosevelt began his third term as president, tensions had been building between the United States and Japan since the early 1930s, when Japan invaded China. The United States had economic and political interests in China and was concerned about this Japanese aggression. As a result, the United States cut off oil supplies to resource-poor Japan. Then, in 1941, Japan allied itself with Nazi Germany and the other Axis powers. The United States supported the opposing side—the Allies—but was still attempting to stay out of the war. Most Americans did not want to get involved in the conflicts overseas.

Shortly before 8:00 a.m. on December 7, 1941, Japanese air forces attacked ships and military buildings in Pearl Harbor, Hawaii, and other bases around the Pacific. The United States had been attempting peace talks with the Japanese at that time, so the attacks were unexpected.

The assault on Pearl Harbor lasted less than two hours. In that short time, the Japanese succeeded in destroying many of the US battleships anchored in the harbor, as well as more than 180 aircraft. The attacks left 2,403 Americans dead. Most of these casualties were sailors, but 68 of them were civilians. Additionally, a total of 1,178 people, including both military personnel and civilians, were wounded during the attack.

The Japanese attacks left Americans shocked and angered. Many people who had been against getting involved in the conflict now changed their minds. The day after the attack, Roosevelt addressed the nation.

A Devastating Attack

Roosevelt begins his speech with its most famous line:

> *Yesterday, December 7, 1941—a date which will live in infamy—the United States of America was suddenly and deliberately*

attacked by naval and air forces of the
Empire of Japan.[1]

He goes on to explain that before this attack, the United States had been pursuing peace talks with the Japanese government and its emperor. According to Roosevelt, one hour after the attack started, the Japanese ambassador to the United States had replied to a message the United States had sent. The message explained Japan now believed it was useless to continue peace talks. However, Roosevelt says, the message had not been openly threatening, nor did it hint at the attacks.

Roosevelt goes on to explain that it is clear Japan's attack on Pearl Harbor was premeditated. He says the distance between Japan and Hawaii proves the attack had to have been planned in advance. He also argues Japan had only pretended to be interested in peace so the United States would not expect this attack.

Under Attack

Next, Roosevelt discusses the damage the attack has caused. He tells his listeners US naval and military forces have suffered extreme damage. He regretfully reports many Americans have died in the attack. Roosevelt also explains Japan's attack on Pearl Harbor was just one part of a larger surprise attack throughout the Pacific.

He notes on the same day as the Pearl Harbor attack, Japan also attacked Malaya (now part of Malaysia). Then, overnight, Japan attacked Hong Kong, Guam, the Philippine Islands, and Wake Island. In the morning, Japan attacked Midway Island. Roosevelt summarizes these attacks to conclude that Japan has performed a large-scale attack throughout the Pacific area.

Call to Action

After he has finished explaining the nature of Japan's attack, Roosevelt calls for the United States to immediately ramp up its efforts to protect itself. He says the American people will never forget the damage done by Japan. There is no doubt Roosevelt wants the United States to take action against its aggressors. He stresses the United States will win against Japan.

Roosevelt believes it is the will of the American people and government that the United States be armed against Japan to ensure such an attack will never happen again. Roosevelt further confirms the

obvious conflict existing between the United States and Japan. He says the United States is in danger of additional Japanese attacks. But Roosevelt places his confidence in the armed forces and the determination of Americans, both of which he believes will lead the country to victory. In the final lines of his speech, Roosevelt asks Congress to declare war on Japan.

Roosevelt's speech was successful; Congress declared war on Japan, and Roosevelt signed the war declaration just hours after the speech's conclusion.

Soon after the Pearl Harbor attack, a series of posters encouraged Americans to buy war bonds to support the war effort.

No.2

How to Apply Listener-Response Criticism to "A Date Which Will Live in Infamy"

What Is Listener-Response Criticism?

Listener-response criticism recognizes that listeners make sense of a speech for themselves while they are reading or listening to it. Listener-response critics acknowledge that listeners do not merely passively accept the information or speech they are hearing, but rather they relate it to their own opinions and experiences. Listeners automatically interpret the meaning of a speech for themselves.

While most other critical theories have a very specific framework, listener-response criticism is more flexible. To employ this type of criticism, the critic needs only to consider what she or he thinks about the work. The critic can make a personal claim about the work and then back it up with examples from the speech or even with personal experiences.

Applying Listener-Response Criticism to "A Date Which Will Live in Infamy"

Roosevelt's famous speech, delivered on December 8, 1941, marked a significant moment in history. The Japanese had just attacked Pearl Harbor and several other sites in the Pacific. Many American lives were lost, and substantial damage was done to military resources. As the leader of a nation previously devoted to maintaining peace and still shaken from the attack, Roosevelt needed to console Americans. He also had to convey the importance of fighting back against the country's enemies. To Roosevelt, war was now the only answer and the only response to Japan's aggression. Roosevelt's speech on December 8, 1941, is composed to convince his listeners that war against Japan is the only possible course of action.

Thesis Statement

At the end of the first paragraph, the author states the thesis: "Roosevelt's speech on December 8, 1941, is composed to convince his listeners that war against Japan is the only possible course of action." In this essay, the author proves her assertion that Roosevelt's speech presents war against Japan as the only option for the United States.

The beginning of Roosevelt's speech is important to its overall structure. Roosevelt gives Americans only one option: war. However, he is careful to ease into the subject of using US military force. <u>Roosevelt begins his speech by discussing peace, presenting the United States as an unsuspecting victim in the attack in an attempt to gain further compassion from the audience.</u> The composition of the first part of the speech makes it clear the United States was the peaceful victim of an unprovoked and purposeful attack by the Japanese. Just a few sentences into the speech, Roosevelt explains, "The United States was at peace with [Japan]" and "looking toward the maintenance of peace in the Pacific."[1] In only one sentence, Roosevelt uses the word *peace* twice. He is reminding Americans that the United States has been a peaceful country and the attack by Japan is the reason that peace is now broken. It seems important to Roosevelt that his listeners view the attack as unprovoked. He says the United States

> **Argument One**
> The first argument states: "Roosevelt begins his speech by discussing peace, presenting the United States as an unsuspecting victim in the attack in an attempt to gain further compassion from the audience." The author proves Roosevelt employs these techniques to gain his audience's sympathy.

was given no warning of the attack by the Japanese. In fact, the attack had to have been planned by Japan for some time due to the distance between the two nations. Yet the Japanese had misled the United States into thinking there could still be peace between the two countries. Roosevelt explains, "The Japanese government has deliberately sought to deceive the United States by false statements and expressions of hope for continued peace."[2] Roosevelt presents the United States as a peaceful nation and Japan as dishonest and corrupt.

Next, Roosevelt uses direct, short sentences to convey Japan's military power in an attempt to heighten the American people's concern over this threat. He says:

Last night Japanese forces attacked Hong Kong.

Last night Japanese forces attacked Guam.

Last night Japanese forces attacked the Philippine Islands.

Argument Two

Next, the author looks at how Roosevelt structures his language in order to heighten his audience's fear of Japan and concern for the United States' future. The second argument is: "Next, Roosevelt uses direct, short sentences to convey Japan's military power in an attempt to heighten the American people's concern over this threat."

Last night Japanese forces attacked
Wake Island.

And this morning the Japanese attacked
Midway Island.[3]

Roosevelt could have simply listed the areas affected by Japan's offensive in one sentence. Instead, he structures the speech so each attack is mentioned in its own sentence. For the reader or listener, this gives each sentence more emphasis and meaning. Roosevelt also builds each sentence in the same way, continually repeating the phrase "Japanese forces attacked" as he lists off the areas that were hit.[4] This repetitive structure makes the speech dramatic. It also helps drive home Roosevelt's point. The Japanese had planned and carried out calculated, deliberate attacks throughout the Pacific. However, Roosevelt does not provide statistics concerning damages or fatalities in those places. Listing the attacks in this way while leaving the details vague may actually make the threat of Japan's military seem worse to the listener or reader than it actually was.

These short sentences also reinforce the fear many Americans were feeling after the surprise attack on Pearl Harbor. By drawing out each

People gather around a Waikiki, Hawaii, store destroyed in the attacks. Americans across the country were shocked by the assault on Hawaii.

separate attack into its own sentence, Roosevelt puts emphasis on the power of Japan and encourages listeners to fear this force. At the end of the repetitive sentences, Roosevelt makes his final point of the section: "Japan has therefore undertaken a surprise offensive extending throughout the Pacific area. The facts of yesterday and today speak for themselves."[5] These statements confirm his listeners' fears. Roosevelt leads the listener to his point of view, affirming he is not creating reasons to go to war. He then points out the facts that make war the only possible course of action. Finally,

Roosevelt provides the real reason for his speech in the final paragraphs: the United States has no choice but to declare war on Japan.

Roosevelt has already presented the United States as peaceful and undeserving of aggression. He has also heightened his listeners' fears about the Japanese empire and its military forces. <u>Roosevelt ends his speech with direct statements, stated as facts, to affirm the need for a declaration of war.</u> Roosevelt does not discuss the real reason for his speech—to ask Congress to declare war on Japan—until near the speech's end. He first hints at his belief that the United States will surely win a fight against Japan, planting the seed that there is now no other course of action open to the United States. After listing the attacks, he notes, "The American people in their righteous might will win through to absolute victory."[6] By speaking as if the nation is already at war before actually mentioning war in his speech, Roosevelt leaves little room for any other opinions. He then makes factual statements affirming the necessity

> **Argument Three**
>
> The author presents the third argument: "Roosevelt ends his speech with direct statements, stated as facts, to affirm the need for a declaration of war." The author explains how Roosevelt uses factual language to promote the need for war.

of this course of action. For example, Roosevelt states simply, "Hostilities exist."[7] This short, direct statement leaves little space for doubt in listeners' minds about whether the nation should go to war. Roosevelt also stresses, "Our people, our territory, and our interests are in grave danger."[8] This statement makes the Japanese threat seem very large indeed.

Conclusion
The conclusion is the final paragraph of a critique. In the conclusion, the author summarizes the argument, now backed up by supporting arguments. She explains Roosevelt's objective is to gain support for his declaration of war by presenting it as the only course of action.

By the time Roosevelt finally requests that Congress declare war against Japan in the speech's last sentence, he has worked hard to prove war is the only possible course of action. The speech is laid out in such a way that the listener or reader is easily persuaded to the president's point of view. The approach worked. Public opinion supporting the war rose immediately after the attack on Pearl Harbor, and just one day after the attack—the same day as Roosevelt's speech—Congress declared war on Japan.

Thinking Critically about "A Date Which Will Live in Infamy"

Now it is your turn to assess the critique. Consider these questions:

1. The author argues Roosevelt's speech is designed to persuade the nation to support the use of military force against Japan. Do you agree? Why or why not?

2. Would you add anything to this argument to make it stronger? Would you take anything out?

3. A conclusion should summarize a critique's thesis statement and supporting arguments and leave the reader with a new idea. Is this conclusion effective? Why or why not?

Other Approaches

As with all types of criticism, there is more than one way to apply listener-response criticism to Roosevelt's "A Date Which Will Live in Infamy" speech. The following are two other approaches that could be applied to this speech using listener-response criticism. The first approach deals with the way the listener feels when hearing this speech today, decades after Roosevelt presented it. The second is a reflection on how Roosevelt promotes national unity and hope throughout the speech.

National Pride Then and Now

Roosevelt's speech following the attack on Pearl Harbor was written and delivered more than half a century ago. However, listeners today can still relate to some of his claims about the United States. In comparison with current struggles faced by the United States, it is clear not much has changed since World War II when it comes to national pride. Many people are still focused on promoting the mission and history of the United States as a world power.

A thesis statement that uses listener-response criticism to address this issue might be: Roosevelt's speech after the attack on Pearl Harbor resonates with a modern listener, revealing that the feeling of national pride promoted in the 1940s still exists today.

A Positive Message

Although the United States had just suffered its most crippling attack since the nation was formed, Roosevelt's speech is not all negative. In fact, Roosevelt attempts to empower US citizens and leave them with a positive message during one of their darkest times. Although the situation is bleak, Roosevelt is optimistic about the nation's ability to win a war against Japan.

A thesis statement for a critique that takes this approach might be: Speaking in the wake of one of the biggest disasters in US history, Roosevelt manages to leave American listeners with a message of hope and endurance.

You Critique It

Now that you have learned about different critical theories and how to apply them to different works, are you ready to perform your own critique? You have read that this type of evaluation can help you look at books, speeches, and essays in new ways and make you pay attention to certain issues you may not have otherwise recognized. So, why not use one of the critical theories profiled in this book to consider a fresh take on your favorite work?

First, choose a theory and the work you want to analyze. Remember that the theory is a springboard for asking questions about the work.

Next, write a specific question that relates to the theory you have selected. Then you can form your thesis, which should provide the answer to that question. Your thesis is the most important part of your critique and offers an argument about the work based on the tenets, or beliefs, of the theory you are applying. Recall that the thesis statement typically appears at the very end of the introductory paragraph of your essay. It is usually only one sentence long.

After you have written your thesis, find evidence to back it up. Good places to start are in the work itself or in journals or articles that discuss what other people have said about it. If you are critiquing a speech, you may also want to read about the speaker's life so you can get a sense of what factors may have affected the creation of the speech. This can be especially useful if working within historical or biographical criticism.

Depending on which theory you are applying, you can often find evidence in the work's language, structure, or historical context. You should also explore parts of the work that seem to disprove your thesis and create an argument against them. As you do this, you might want to address what other critics have written about the work. Their quotes may help support your claim.

Before you start analyzing a work, think about the different arguments made in this book. Reflect on how evidence supporting the thesis was presented. Did you find that some of the techniques used to back up the arguments were more convincing than others? Try these methods as you prove your thesis in your own critique.

When you are finished writing your critique, read it over carefully. Is your thesis statement understandable? Do the supporting arguments flow logically, with the topic of each paragraph clearly stated? Can you add any information that would present your readers with a stronger argument in favor of your thesis? Were you able to use quotes from the work, as well as from other critics, to enhance your ideas?

Did you see the work in a new light?

Timeline

1882
Franklin Delano Roosevelt is born on January 30 in Hyde Park, New York.

1896
Roosevelt enrolls in Groton, a boarding school for boys in Massachusetts.

1920
Roosevelt runs for vice president with presidential hopeful James Cox, but Cox loses the election.

1921
Roosevelt is stricken with polio during a family vacation in August; his legs become paralyzed.

1924
Emerging from ongoing treatment for his paralysis, Roosevelt speaks at the Democratic National Convention.

1928
Roosevelt is elected governor of New York. He is reelected in 1930.

1929
The stock market crashes, setting off the Great Depression.

1932
Roosevelt is elected president of the United States; he begins implementing his New Deal programs.

1936
An overwhelming majority of voters reelect Roosevelt for a second term as president.

1900 — Roosevelt enrolls at Harvard University.

1904 — Roosevelt enrolls at Columbia Law School.

1905 — On March 17, Roosevelt marries Anna Eleanor Roosevelt.

1910 — Roosevelt is elected to the New York State Senate.

1913 — President Wilson appoints Roosevelt assistant secretary of the navy.

1940 — Roosevelt is elected for a third term as president.

1941 — On December 7, Japanese forces carry out a surprise attack on Pearl Harbor, Hawaii, and other Pacific bases; at Roosevelt's urging, the United States declares war on Japan on December 8.

1945 — On April 12, Roosevelt dies after suffering a cerebral hemorrhage; World War II ends on September 2.

Glossary

adversity
Misfortune or hardship.

depression
A decrease in economic activity.

ideology
Social belief.

imagery
A mental picture portrayed through text, often metaphorically.

inaugural
Relating to the induction into office.

neutral
Unbiased.

offensive
An attack.

paralyzed
Unable to move.

personify
To give something human characteristics.

prejudice
An opinion based on preconceived ideas rather than facts.

prevalent
Widely accepted.

regulate
To control.

stigma
   A social opinion that something is unacceptable.

sustainable
   Maintainable.

Bibliography of Works and Criticism

Important Works

"Fear Itself" Speech, March 4, 1933

"On the Bank Crisis" Fireside Chat, March 12, 1933

"On Drought Conditions" Fireside Chat, September 6, 1936

"The Forces of Selfishness and of Lust for Power Met Their Match" Speech, October 31, 1936

"The Arsenal of Democracy" Speech, December 29, 1940

"Four Freedoms" Speech, January 6, 1941

"A Date Which Will Live in Infamy" Speech, December 8, 1941

"Report on the Home Front" Fireside Chat, October 12, 1942

Essential Critiques

Critical Discussions

Bronner, Stephen Eric. *Critical Theory: A Very Short Introduction*. Oxford, UK: Oxford UP, 2011. Print.

Houck, Davis W. *FDR and Fear Itself: The First Inaugural Address*. College Station, TX: Texas A&M UP, 2002. Print.

Rosmaita, Gregory J. "The Four Freedoms, At Home and Abroad." *An American Exegesis*. Gregory J. Rosmaita, n.d. Web. 23 May 2012.

Yu, Lumeny. "The Great Communicator: How FDR's Radio Speeches Shaped American History." *The History Teacher*. History Cooperative, Nov. 2005. Web. 23 May 2012.

Resources

Selected Bibliography

Black, Conrad. *Franklin Delano Roosevelt: Champion of Freedom*. New York: PublicAffairs, 2003. Print.

Golway, Terry. *Together We Cannot Fail: FDR and the American Presidency in Years of Crisis*. Naperville, IL: SourceBooks MediaFusion, 2009. Print.

"On Drought Conditions." *Fireside Chats of Franklin D. Roosevelt*. Franklin D. Roosevelt, Presidential Library and Museum, n.d. Web. 6 Aug. 2012.

MacArthur, Brian, ed. "Franklin D. Roosevelt: 'The Only Thing to Fear Is Fear Itself.'" *The Penguin Book of Twentieth Century Speeches*. New York: Penguin, 1999. Print.

Further Readings

Pederson, William D. *The FDR Years*. New York: Facts on File, 2006. Print.

Vander Hook, Sue. *The Dust Bowl*. Edina, MN: ABDO, 2009. Print.

Vander Hook, Sue. *Franklin D. Roosevelt: 32nd U.S. President*. Edina, MN: ABDO, 2008. Print.

Web Links

To learn more about critiquing the speeches of Franklin D. Roosevelt, visit ABDO Publishing Company online at **www.abdopublishing.com**. Web sites about the works of Franklin D. Roosevelt are featured on our Book Links page. These links are routinely monitored and updated to provide the most current information available.

For More Information

Franklin D. Roosevelt Presidential Library and Museum
4079 Albany Post Road, Hyde Park, NY 12538
1-800-FDR-VISIT
www.fdrlibrary.marist.edu

This museum and its library were built under Roosevelt's direction and opened in 1941. Today the library promotes research on Franklin and Eleanor Roosevelt.

National World War II Museum
945 Magazine Street, New Orleans, LA 70130
504-528-1944
www.nationalww2museum.org

This museum presents artifacts from World War II. Films about the war and music from that time period can also be enjoyed here.

Source Notes

Chapter 1. Introduction to Critiques
None.

Chapter 2. A Closer Look at Franklin D. Roosevelt
None.

Chapter 3. An Overview of "Fear Itself"

1. Brian MacArthur, ed. "Franklin D. Roosevelt: 'The Only Thing to Fear Is Fear Itself.'" *The Penguin Book of Twentieth Century Speeches*. New York: Penguin, 1999. Print. 128.

2. Ibid. 129.

Chapter 4. How to Apply Biographical Criticism to "Fear Itself"

1. Roy Jenkins. *Franklin Delano Roosevelt*. New York: Times, 2003. Print. 43.

2. "American President: A Reference Resource." *Miller Center*. University of Virginia, n.d. Web. 3 May 2012.

3. Brian MacArthur, ed. "Franklin D. Roosevelt: 'The Only Thing to Fear Is Fear Itself.'" *The Penguin Book of Twentieth Century Speeches*. New York: Penguin, 1999. Print. 128.

4. "F.D.R.'s First Inaugural Speech: Nothing to Fear." *YouTube*. YouTube, 28 Aug. 2009. Web. 10 June 2012.

5. Ibid.

6. Brian MacArthur, ed. "Franklin D. Roosevelt: 'The Only Thing to Fear Is Fear Itself.'" *The Penguin Book of Twentieth Century Speeches*. New York: Penguin, 1999. Print. 129.

7. Ibid. 129.

8. Ibid. 131.

9. Jonathan Alter. *The Defining Moment: FDR's Hundred Days and the Triumph of Hope*. New York: Simon & Schuster, 2006. Print. 64.

10. Brian MacArthur, ed. "Franklin D. Roosevelt: 'The Only Thing to Fear Is Fear Itself.'" *The Penguin Book of Twentieth Century Speeches*. New York: Penguin, 1999. Print. 128–129.

Chapter 5. An Overview of "On Drought Conditions"

1. "On Drought Conditions." *Fireside Chats of Franklin D. Roosevelt*. Franklin D. Roosevelt, Presidential Library and Museum, n.d. Web. 26 Apr. 2012.

Chapter 6. How to Apply Marxist Criticism to "On Drought Conditions"

1. "On Drought Conditions." *Fireside Chats of Franklin D. Roosevelt*. Franklin D. Roosevelt, Presidential Library and Museum, n.d. Web. 3 May 2012.

2. Ibid.

3. Ibid.

4. Ibid.

Chapter 7. An Overview of "Four Freedoms"

1. Brian MacArthur, ed. "Franklin Delano Roosevelt: 'The Four Freedoms.'" *The Penguin Book of Twentieth Century Speeches*. New York: Penguin, 1999. Print. 199.

2. Ibid.

3. Ibid.

4. Ibid. 200.

5. Ibid.

6. Ibid. 201.

7. Ibid.

8. Ibid. 202.

Chapter 8. How to Apply Rhetorical Criticism to "Four Freedoms"

1. Brian MacArthur, ed. "Franklin Delano Roosevelt: 'The Four Freedoms.'" *The Penguin Book of Twentieth Century Speeches*. New York: Penguin, 1999. Print. 200.

2. Ibid.

3. Ibid.

4. Ibid. 202.

5. Ibid.

6. Ibid.

7. Ibid.

8. Ibid.

9. Ibid. 199.

Chapter 9. An Overview of "A Date Which Will Live in Infamy"

1. Brian MacArthur, ed. "Franklin Delano Roosevelt: 'A Date Which Will Live in Infamy.'" *The Penguin Book of Twentieth Century Speeches*. New York: Penguin, 1999. Print. 207.

Chapter 10. How to Apply Listener-Response Criticism to "A Date Which Will Live in Infamy"

1. Brian MacArthur, ed. "Franklin Delano Roosevelt: 'A Date Which Will Live in Infamy.'" *The Penguin Book of Twentieth Century Speeches*. New York: Penguin, 1999. Print. 207.

2. Ibid.

3. Ibid.

4. Ibid.

5. Ibid.

6. Ibid. 208.

7. Ibid.

8. Ibid.

Index

"A Date Which Will Live in
Infamy," 79–83, 85–95
Allied powers, 18–19, 79
arguments, how to write, 10,
96–97
Aristotle, 68, 69, 76, 77
Axis powers, 18, 62, 74, 79

biographical criticism, 7–8, 9,
29–39
conclusion, 36
evidence and arguments,
31–36
other approaches, 38–39
thesis statement, 31, 38–39

Campobello Island, Maine, 15
Congress, 18, 26, 27, 61, 63, 83,
91, 92,
Cox, James, 15
critical theory, definitions of,
6–9
biographical, 29
listener response, 85–86
Marxist, 49
rhetorical, 67–68

Democratic National
Convention, 16
dust bowl, 42–43

Employment Service, 46
ethos, 68, 76
evidence, how to use, 9, 96–97

"Fear Itself," 21–27, 29–39
fireside chats, 41, 42–43, 46, 50,
54, 56–57
"Four Freedoms," 59–65, 67–77

Great Depression, 13, 16, 17,
21–27, 30, 36, 41–42, 49–51,
53, 54, 56, 57

Howe, Louis, 16

Japan, 18–19, 79, 80, 81, 82, 83,
86–91, 92, 95

Labor Day, 45–46, 47, 53
listener-response criticism,
85–95
conclusion, 92
evidence and arguments,
87–92
other approaches, 94–95
thesis statement, 86, 94–95
logos, 68, 69

Marx, Karl, 49
Marxist criticism, 49–57
    conclusion, 54
    evidence and arguments,
        51–54
    other approaches, 56–57
    thesis statement, 50, 57
Moley, Raymond, 21, 29

New Deal, 17, 50

"On Drought Conditions,"
    42–47, 49–57

pathos, 68, 69
Pearl Harbor, Hawaii, 18, 79–80,
    81, 82, 86, 89, 92, 94

rhetorical criticism, 67–77
    conclusion, 74
    evidence and arguments,
        69–74
    other approaches, 76–77
    thesis statement, 69, 76, 77
Roosevelt, Anna Eleanor (wife),
    14, 16, 31

Roosevelt, Franklin
    childhood, 13–14
    death, 18
    education, 14
    inauguration, 21, 30, 31, 35,
        36, 38, 39
    optimistic, 33, 34, 38–39, 95
    polio, 15–16, 30–31, 34, 35,
        36
    politics, 14–15, 16–17, 39
    presidency, 17–19, 21, 25, 27,
        30, 34, 36, 41, 59, 61, 76,
        77, 79
    religion, 39
    speeches (overview), 21–27,
        42–47, 59–65, 79–83
Roosevelt, James (father), 13
Roosevelt, Sara (mother), 13

thesis statement, how to write,
    9–10, 96–97

Warm Springs, Georgia, 16
World War II, 13, 17–19, 59, 60,
    61, 62, 69, 74, 79, 83, 86–87,
    91, 92, 94, 95

About the Author

Mari Kesselring is the author and editor of many fiction and nonfiction books for young people.

Photo Credits